ALAN SHEARER

A BIOGRAPHY

aydn Middleton

For Andrew and Calum, who know a good
player when they see one! H.M.

Heinemann Educational Publishers
Halley Court, Jordan Hill, Oxford OX2 8EJ
a division of Reed Educational & Professional Publishing Limited

Heinemann is a registered trademark of Reed Educational & Professional
Publishing Limited

OXFORD MELBOURNE AUCKLAND
JOHANNESBURG BLANTYRE GABORONE
IBADAN PORTSMOUTH (NH) USA CHICAGO

First published 1999

03 02 01 00 99
10 9 8 7 6 5 4 3 2

British Library Cataloguing in Publication Data
A catalogue record for this book is available from the British Library.

ISBN 0 435 09683 4 *A Biography of Alan Shearer* single copy
ISBN 0 435 09684 2 *A Biography of Alan Shearer* 6 copy pack

Photos: Action Images, pages 4, 8, 19. Rex Features, page 6. Empics Ltd / Don Morley, page
9. Rex Features / The Sun, page 10. Football Archive / Peter Robinson, pages 13, 18, 22, 23.
Empics Ltd, pages 15, 16, 21, 25, 26, 27. Laurence Griffiths / Empics Ltd, page 20. Empics
Ltd / Michael Steele, page 28. Allsport, page 29.

Designed by M2
Printed and bound in the UK

Contents

THERE'S ONLY ONE ALAN SHEARER

For lovers of English football, 1966 was a special year because England won the World Cup. For the next four years they reigned as world champions until, in June 1970, Brazil took their crown. Two months after that, in the north-east of England, a baby boy was born. He grew up to be a brilliant footballer and, at the age of 26, he was made captain of England. His name was Alan Shearer and he had only one aim: to lead his country to victory in the World Cup for a second time.

Today's top footballers make huge fortunes, but down-to-earth Alan knows how crazy that can be. He says, 'Compared with people like doctors and nurses and others who are not properly rewarded for the vital work they do, we are massively overpaid.'

The big man

Alan is England's best striker of the 1990s. Everything about him is big – from the number of goals he scores to the size of his transfer fees. In 1992 he was transferred from his first club, Southampton, to Blackburn Rovers for the huge sum of £3.3 million. But his new manager, Kenny Dalglish, still thought he had a bargain. 'Shearer lifts the entire team and turns draws into victories,' he said. 'He's priceless.'

Four years later – just after he had won the Golden Boot as top scorer in the European Championship of 1996 – Alan was transferred from Blackburn to Newcastle United for £15 million. Someone worked out that this was 22 times his own weight in gold! Alan has become a rich man through football, but he still has a boy's love of the game.

'I honestly don't think that it's possible for him to train or play at 75%,' says ex-footballer Glenn Roeder. 'He is the type of person who has to give 100% all the time.' Managers like that – and so do fans.

WORLD CUP WINNERS

1930	Uruguay	1970	Brazil
1934	Italy	1974	West Germany
1938	Italy	1978	Argentina
1950	Uruguay	1982	Italy
1954	West Germany	1986	Argentina
1958	Brazil	1990	Germany
1962	Brazil	1994	Brazil
1966	England	1998	France

Kevin Keegan, Alan's boyhood hero, who thrilled Newcastle United fans with his skills in the early 1980s.

GEORDIE BOY

Alan is a 'Geordie', the nickname for people who come from Newcastle. He was born in the Gosforth district of the city on 13 August 1970. 'As a lad,' he recalls, 'I played football every day, sometimes with a can or a stone if I couldn't find a proper ball.' His father, a sheet metal worker, was a passionate fan of the local football club, Newcastle United.

Alan too became a keen supporter. His boyhood idol was Kevin Keegan, an ex-England captain who joined the Magpies in 1982. Two years later, Kevin inspired Newcastle to promotion from the Second Division to the First. (Before 1992, there was no Premier League. The top division was called Division One.) Alan dreamed of following in Kevin's footsteps as a Newcastle United striker. Many years later, Kevin would help to make that dream come true.

Determined to succeed

While at school in Gosforth, Alan played a lot of football. Outside school, he also played for Wallsend Boys Club and Cramlington Juniors, scoring goals by the dozen. When he was only 15, he starred in the Northumberland Boys Under-19 county team. His childhood ambition was to be a professional footballer, but he had three drawbacks. Firstly, he was small for his age; secondly, he was not a very fast runner; and thirdly, he could not kick very well with his left foot. His father says that this did not bother Alan: 'No one and nothing was going to stop him... He refused even to consider the possibility of failure.'

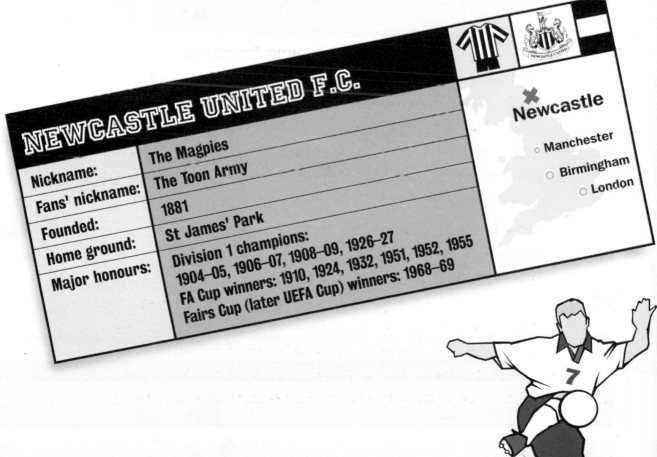

NEWCASTLE UNITED F.C.

Nickname:	The Magpies
Fans' nickname:	The Toon Army
Founded:	1881
Home ground:	St James' Park
Major honours:	Division 1 champions: 1904–05, 1906–07, 1908–09, 1926–27
	FA Cup winners: 1910, 1924, 1932, 1951, 1952, 1955
	Fairs Cup (later UEFA Cup) winners: 1968–69

Newcastle

○ Manchester

○ Birmingham

○ London

Matthew Le Tissier – one of several young Saints who would go on to great things.

THE SAINT

Big professional football clubs have 'scouts' in many parts of the country. These are men who watch boys' matches and try to spot the stars of the future. Scouts from several clubs thought that Alan was a promising striker. One, Jack Hixon, thought that he could be great. 'He had a good football brain,' he says 'and he had all three of what I call the essential fundamentals: attitude, application and character.'

Jack arranged for Alan to have a trial for his club – Southampton – and in 1984 they signed him as an associate schoolboy. This meant that when he left school two years later, Southampton would have the first chance to sign him as a trainee professional.

SOUTHAMPTON F.C.	
Nickname:	The Saints
Founded:	1885
Home ground:	The Dell
Major honours:	Division 1 runners-up: 1983–84 FA Cup winners: 1976

○ Manchester
○ Birmingham
○ London
✖ **Southampton**

Going south

In 1984 the Saints were one of the top clubs in England. Alan did not care that the place was 300 miles away from home. In 1986, just before his sixteenth birthday, he was signed as a trainee, and had to move to lodgings on the south coast. But 'he was never homesick,' according to Dave Merrington, the Southampton youth team coach.

In his two seasons as a youth team player Alan trained hard and he grew bigger, stronger and more skilful – even with his left foot; and he kept on scoring goals – more than 75 of them. His young team mates called him Smokey because he was so keen on Smokey Bacon crisps. He was not as naturally talented as another Southampton youngster – Matthew Le Tissier. But, as Jack Hixon predicted, 'he will always make the most of what he's got,' and before he was eighteen he was good enough to play in the first team.

One of Southampton's older stars was Peter Shilton, who won a record 125 caps for England.

In 1991, Alan married Lainya Arnold. Their first daughter, Chloe, was born in 1992.

HAT-TRICK HERO

Southampton were not doing well in the 1987–8 season. Meanwhile, Alan was scoring regularly for the youth team. Dave Merrington was sure that he could score at any level, so on 8 April 1988 Alan made his full debut for the first team. The opponents that afternoon were mighty Arsenal, but within 49 minutes Alan had scored three times.

His two headers and a shot helped Southampton to win 4–2. At the age of seventeen years and 240 days, he was the youngest ever player to score a hat-trick in the top division. He was given the match ball as a souvenir, autographed by all the players. He was also told that it was his turn to get the kit washed that weekend. But his kit-washing days would soon be over. Four days after scoring his hat-trick, he signed for Southampton as a full-time professional footballer.

Shearer's League goal record at Southampton 1987–1992.

SEASON	APPEARANCES	GOALS
1987–88	8 appearances	3 goals
1988–89	10 appearances	0 goals
1989–90	26 appearances	3 goals
1990–91	36 appearances	4 goals
1991–92	41 appearances	13 goals

Goal trickle

In each of the next four seasons, Alan played more games for Southampton's first team. He scored only twenty goals in that time, but as his team mate Jason Dodd said, 'You also need people to make the right runs off the ball and unsettle defences, and this is where Alan was so highly valued in that team.' He became very popular with the Southampton fans, who voted him their Player of the Year in 1991. They recognized a whole-hearted, unselfish team player when they saw one – and so did the coaches of the England Under-21 squad...

THREE LIONS ON HIS SHIRT

While he was still kicking stones and cans in Gosforth, the young Alan Shearer had big plans. 'My ambition was the same as practically every boy in Newcastle,' he says. 'To play for England.' His moment came in 1987, when he made his first full appearance for England's Under-17 side against the Republic of Ireland – and scored. Three years later came his debut for the under-21s, once again against the Republic of Ireland, and this time he scored twice. Within a year he was captaining the England Under-21 team and, at an international tournament in Toulon, France, he led his country to victory, scoring seven goals in four games.

England's performances in the final stages of European Championships and World Cups since Alan Shearer was born.

DATE	CHAMPIONSHIP	RESULT
1970	World Cup	Quarter finals
1972	European Championships	Quarter finals
1974	World Cup	Did not qualify
1976	European Championships	Did not qualify
1978	World Cup	Did not qualify
1980	European Championships	First round
1982	World Cup	Second round
1984	European Championships	Did not qualify
1986	World Cup	Quarter finals
1988	European Championships	First round
1990	World Cup	Semi finals
1992	European Championships	First round
1994	World Cup	Did not qualify
1996	European Championships	Semi finals
1998	World Cup	Second round

Getting better all the time

Meanwhile, the full England team, under manager Graham Taylor, was busy qualifying for the 1992 European Championships. Several young strikers were chosen to play in friendly matches before Euro '92. Alan was one of them. At Wembley, on 19 February 1992, he won his first senior cap for England, scoring the first goal in a 2–0 win against France. Although he was then picked for the Euro '92 squad, he played in only one game, and England were knocked out without winning a match.

Nevertheless, his Southampton manager Ian Branfoot believed that he was on the verge of great things: 'He is a grafter who is full of aggression and enthusiasm for his work. Not only this, he absorbs things very quickly... With Alan, you only have to tell him once and he does it. So if you think he's a good player now, just wait – he's going to be an awful lot better.'

Alan making his 1992 England debut against France.

13

RECORD BREAKER

In July 1992, after six years at Southampton, Alan moved back to the north of England. His new club was Blackburn Rovers, whose wealthy chairman, Jack Walker, had told manager Kenny Dalglish to buy the best centre-forward in England – no matter what he cost. Almost everyone now agreed that Alan was England's top striker, but was he worth the British transfer record fee of £3.3 million that Blackburn had to pay? If he helped Blackburn to win the new Premier League, then people would believe that he was.

A report in Southampton's *Evening Echo* newspaper said that 'he has a massive weight on his shoulders, but he starts with his new club knowing that he has this city's best wishes going with him. Alan Shearer has always conducted himself well, and has shown a maturity beyond his years.' Southampton's fans were going to miss him badly.

BLACKBURN ROVERS F.C.

Nickname:	Rovers
Founded:	1875
Home ground:	Ewood Park
Major honours:	Premiership Champions: 1994–95 Division 1 champions: 1911–12, 1913–14 FA Cup winners: 1884, 1885, 1890, 1891, 1928

Blackburn
Manchester
Birmingham
London

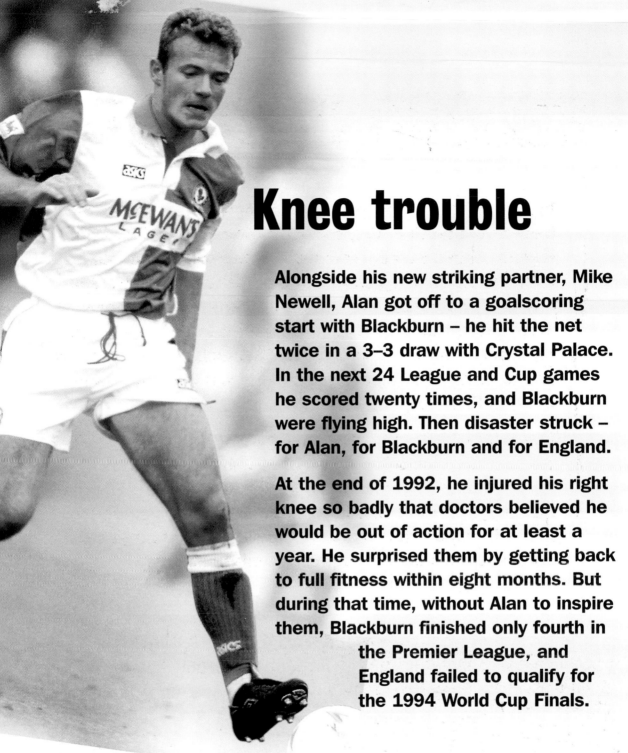

Knee trouble

Alongside his new striking partner, Mike Newell, Alan got off to a goalscoring start with Blackburn – he hit the net twice in a 3–3 draw with Crystal Palace. In the next 24 League and Cup games he scored twenty times, and Blackburn were flying high. Then disaster struck – for Alan, for Blackburn and for England.

At the end of 1992, he injured his right knee so badly that doctors believed he would be out of action for at least a year. He surprised them by getting back to full fitness within eight months. But during that time, without Alan to inspire them, Blackburn finished only fourth in the Premier League, and England failed to qualify for the 1994 World Cup Finals.

Alan in action for Blackburn, 1992.

15

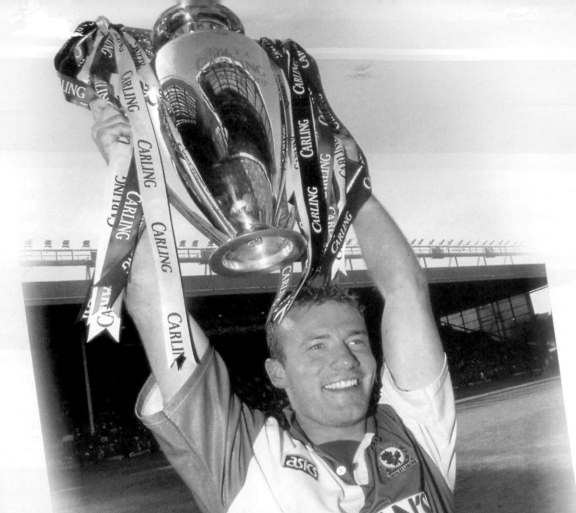

CHAMPIONS!

The team that won the Premier League in 1992–93 was Manchester United. It was the first time they had won the League since 1966–67. In the next season they repeated the feat, with Blackburn Rovers finishing second and Alan, back from injury, scoring 31 League goals.

Besides Alan, Blackburn now had several other expensive star players: Tim Flowers, David Batty, Paul Warhurst and new goalscorer Chris Sutton. The Shearer and Sutton strike force, or 'SAS' as it was nicknamed, led Blackburn to even greater success in the following season.

The Premier League table at the end of Blackburn's championship season. Only three seasons before, they had been in Division One.

TEAM	HOME				AWAY			POINTS
	P	W	D	L	W	D	L	
Blackburn Rovers	42	17	2	2	10	6	5	89
Manchester United	42	16	4	1	10	6	5	88
Nottingham Forest	42	12	6	3	10	5	6	77
Liverpool	42	13	5	3	8	6	7	74
Leeds	42	13	5	3	7	8	6	73
Newcastle	42	14	6	1	6	6	9	72
Tottenham Hotspur	42	10	5	6	6	9	6	62
Queens Park Rangers	42	11	3	7	6	6	9	60
Wimbledon	42	9	5	7	6	6	9	56
Southampton	42	8	9	4	4	9	8	54

End of the 81 year wait

For most of the 1994–95 campaign, Blackburn headed the table. Thanks to the goals scored by Shearer and Sutton, and a defence that gave away very few goals, it seemed that no one could stop them from winning the championship. But Manchester United pressed them hard. It was not until the last game of the season that the race came to an end – with Blackburn pipping the 'Red Devils' by just one point. Blackburn were champions for the first time since the First World War broke out.

As well as winning his championship medal, Alan was the Premier League's top goalscorer, with 34 goals to his name. Then, to round off a perfect season, he was voted Player of the Year, not only by the Blackburn fans, but also by the Professional Footballers' Association.

GOAL DROUGHT

Despite the achievements of individual strikers like Alan, football is a team game. Even the best strikers depend on other players to supply the passes that lead to goals. In 1994–95 Alan's Blackburn team-mates were extremely good at doing this, and he scored many more goals there than he had at Southampton. Their 'service' to him continued in the 1995–96 season, when he scored another 31 goals, including no fewer than five hat-tricks.

Unfortunately, Blackburn's defensive play was not so good, and they finished only seventh in the League. And, although Alan was scoring regularly for Blackburn, it was a different story when he played for England.

Alan's place in peril?

The European Championship Finals of 1996 were due to be played in England. Since they were the home team, England did not have to qualify, but they played a number of friendly matches to warm up for the tournament. Almost unbelievably, over a period of 21 months, Alan played in twelve games without scoring a goal. Some critical newspaper reporters suggested that Alan should be replaced in Euro '96 by either Newcastle's Les Ferdinand or Liverpool's Robbie Fowler.

But Alan still had two factors in his favour. Firstly, he still believed that he was England's best striker, and secondly, so did manager Terry Venables. So Alan was picked to play in the first match of Euro '96, against Switzerland.

Alan's family always gives him full support, through the good times and the bad.

GOLDEN BOOT

Alan answered his critics by blasting the first goal in a 1–1 draw with Switzerland. The chorus of support grew louder when his header powered England towards a 2–0 victory against Scotland. Even better was to follow: Alan scored twice in a breathtaking 4–1 win against Holland. After that, England were through to the quarter-finals of the tournament, against Spain.

That match ended in a goalless draw, so the result had to be decided by a penalty shoot-out. Alan took the first England kick – just as he took them for Blackburn – and he set England on the way to another victory. In the semi-final, mighty Germany now waited.

Ecstasy and agony

In the third minute of the Germany game, Alan headed home to put England 1–0 up. He had now proved beyond doubt that he could score goals at the highest international level. But Germany soon equalized, then the game ended with no further goals, which meant another penalty shoot-out. But although Alan fired in the first for England, Gareth Southgate missed the sixth. England were knocked out, and Germany went on to win Euro '96.

Alongside the pain of defeat, Alan had the consolation of winning the 'Golden Boot' award for scoring more goals than anyone else in the tournament. Author Shaun Campbell wrote in his 1997 biography of Alan: 'The world was now at his feet. There wasn't a club anywhere that didn't want his name on their team sheet. But there were few, very few indeed, who would be able to afford him.'

Alan celebrating with Paul Gascoigne and Teddy Sheringham en route to the semi-final of Euro '96.

BACK HOME

'Yes, we've got the big one we wanted. This is a signing for the people of Newcastle.'

The speaker was Kevin Keegan, ex-England captain and former Newcastle United star, now manager of the club. The player he had just bought was Alan Shearer, the Geordie boy who had once been thrilled to meet Kevin after winning a newspaper competition. Back then, Newcastle could have signed young Alan for nothing. Now, on 29 July 1996, Blackburn Rovers were making them pay a world record fee of £15 million.

At this press conference, the newly-signed Alan was flanked by Newcastle chairman Sir John Hall and manager Kevin Keegan.

Immediately after Alan's transfer, the Newcastle club shop sold £70,000 worth of replica Newcastle United shirts.

Return of the hero

Thousands of Newcastle fans flocked to St James' Park on the day the transfer was announced. None of them could quite believe the news. For weeks there had been rumours that Alan would join Manchester United or a top foreign club, but in the end he had come back home. Alan had scored 112 goals in 138 games for Blackburn. If he did the same for Newcastle next season, the Magpies would surely challenge champions Manchester United.

He explained his decision to return home this way: 'I wanted to play for Newcastle. Kevin Keegan was a big influence. On one hand I'd always wanted to play for the club and he didn't really have to sell it to me. I knew what it was all about. But on the other hand I was talking to one of my heroes, a man I had paid to watch as a kid.'

RUNNERS UP

Kevin Keegan's Newcastle team of 1996-97 was as talented as it was expensive. Besides Alan there were stars like David Ginola, Faustino Asprilla, Peter Beardsley and Alan's new strike partner Les Ferdinand. They played with such breathtaking attacking flair that soon they became heroes not only to the Newcastle fans, but the second-favourite team of many other clubs' fans too.

Alan's knack for scoring goals did not desert him. Despite more injury problems, he scored 25 times in 31 League games, making him the Premiership's leading marksman once again. Leicester City fans will certainly remember him. Their team was winning 3–1 against Newcastle until Alan took a hand. Scoring a hat-trick in just 13 minutes, he turned defeat into victory. At the season's end he was again voted the PFA Player of the Year, but this time he did not have a championship medal to go with his award.

TEAM	HOME				AWAY			POINTS
	P	W	D	L	W	D	L	
Manchester United	38	12	5	2	9	7	3	75
Newcastle United	38	13	3	3	6	8	5	68
Arsenal	38	10	5	4	9	6	4	68
Liverpool	38	10	6	3	9	5	5	68
Aston Villa	38	11	5	3	6	5	8	61
Chelsea	38	9	8	2	7	3	9	59
Sheffield Wednesday	38	8	10	1	6	5	8	57
Wimbledon	38	9	6	4	6	5	8	56
Leicester City	38	7	5	7	5	6	8	47
Tottenham Hotspur	38	8	4	7	5	3	11	46

The Premier League table at the end of the 1996–97 season. Over the whole season, Manchester United proved a better all-round team than Newcastle United, even though Newcastle beat them 5–0 in one memorable match.

Reunited with King Kenny

Newcastle finished the season as runners-up to Manchester United, and with a different manager from the one they started with. In January 1997 Kevin Keegan had suddenly resigned as the pressure on him to succeed became too great. His replacement was another football idol to millions – Alan's old manager at Blackburn Rovers, Kenny Dalglish.

After leaving St James' Park, Kevin said, 'My proudest achievement was that I brought Alan Shearer home... For years we had local talent leave. Now for the first time we brought some back. And not just any player either. I think we got the greatest of all.' As for Kenny, he just said, 'I'm lost for words when it comes to describing Shearer's achievements.'

Alan failed to score against only three Premiership teams in 1996–97: Middlesborough, West Ham and his old club, Southampton.

Alan is a deeply patriotic Englishman. 'There's not many things that can beat skippering your country,' he says. 'It's a great honour for me.'

CAPTAIN MARVEL

On 1 September 1996 England began to play their qualifying games for the 1998 World Cup Finals. The first match was against Moldova in Chisinau, and leading out the England team that day was... Alan Shearer. 'There is something special about leading your country,' said new England manager Glenn Hoddle, 'and it should fall to special players. Alan is in that category, so you give him the [captain's] armband and hope it gives him even greater power.'

Alan let no one down. In that first game he scored as England won 3–0, and he went on to score four more times in the next four games. Then, at the end of the season, he led England to victory in a friendly tournament in France. It seemed as if things could only get better – for Alan and for England – during the 1997–98 season leading up to the World Cup Finals.

In spite of his best efforts, Alan ended up on the losing side in the 1998 Cup Final against Arsenal.

Injury strikes again

In a pre-season friendly match against Chelsea, Alan injured his fibula and ankle so badly that he put himself out of action until the spring. It was a terrible blow. England managed to qualify for the World Cup Finals without him, but Newcastle faltered badly and finished only thirteenth in the Premiership.

Yet all was not quite lost. Alan returned before the season's end and scored five Cup goals which helped to take Newcastle to their first FA Cup Final since 1974, against Arsenal. With Newcastle 0–1 down, Alan curled a snapshot past Arsenal and England goalkeeper David Seaman, but the ball hit the post. It was not to be Newcastle's day. Arsenal, the new Premiership champions, also went on to win the Cup by two goals to nil.

27

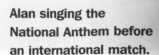
Alan singing the National Anthem before an international match.

PENALTY PAIN – AGAIN!

In June 1998, Alan led out the England team for their first group match in the World Cup Finals in France. Their opponents were Tunisia. Millions of fans all over the world were watching closely. Did Alan's team have the skill and nerve to fulfil his dream and win the World Cup for the first time since 1966?

Just before half time Alan headed a goal from a free kick by his former Blackburn team-mate Graham Le Saux. Late in the second half Paul Scholes scored a second, and the game was won 2–0. Alan and England celebrated, but a shock awaited in their second game – they lost 1–2 to Romania. Now they had to beat Colombia to go through to the second, knockout phase.

A new strike partner

A bright new star lined up alongside Alan against the Colombians: Liverpool's 18-year-old Michael Owen. Some were already calling him 'the next Alan Shearer'. Both of them played well that evening, and England won 2–0. They were through to the second phase. Their next match, against Argentina, would be one of the most memorable so far in Alan's career.

Argentina took an early lead, but then Michael Owen won a penalty. Alan made no mistake from the spot: 1–1. Minutes later, Owen scored a fabulous goal himself, and England kept the lead until just before half-time, when Argentina equalised. The score stayed at 2–2 until the end of extra time.

Just as in the semi-final of Euro '96, there had to be a penalty shoot-out. Just as in Euro '96, Alan made no mistake with his own spot-kick. But again it was not enough. Paul Ince and David Batty failed to score, and England were out of the competition. Alan's dream of glory was over – or put on hold for another four years.

THE FIRST ELEVEN SEASONS

Alan made his top division debut in 1987–88. These statistics show how many club games he has played in since then, and how many goals he has scored. During this time he was also capped 43 times (and scored 20 goals) for England.

For Southampton FC

Year	Competition	Appearances	Goals
1987–88	League	3 (plus 2 as a sub)	3
1988–89	League	8 (2)	0
1989–90	League	19 (7)	3
	FA Cup	1 (0)	0
	Littlewoods Cup	4 (2)	2
	Total	**24 (9)**	**5**
1990–91	League	34 (2)	4
	FA Cup	3 (1)	2
	Rumbelows Cup	6 (0)	6
	ZDS Cup	2 (0)	2
	Total	**45 (3)**	**14**
1991–92	League	41 (0)	13
	FA Cup	7 (0)	2
	Rumbelows Cup	6 (0)	3
	ZDS Cup	6 (0)	3
	Total	**60 (0)**	**21**

For Blackburn Rovers FC

Year	Competition	Appearances	Goals
1992–93	League	21 (0)	16
	Coca-Cola Cup	5 (0)	6
	Total	**26 (0)**	**22**
1993–94	League	34 (6)	31
	FA Cup	4 (0)	2
	Coca-Cola Cup	4 (0)	1
	Total	**42 (6)**	**34**
1994–95	League	42 (0)	34
	FA Cup	2 (0)	0
	Coca-Cola Cup	3 (0)	2
	UEFA Cup	2 (0)	1
	Total	**49 (0)**	**37**
1995–96	League	35 (0)	31
	FA Cup	2 (0)	0
	Coca-Cola Cup	4 (0)	5
	European Cup	6 (0)	1
	Charity Shield	1 (0)	0
	Total	**48 (0)**	**37**

For Newcastle United FC

Year	Competition	Appearances	Goals
1996–97	League	31 (0)	25
	FA Cup	3 (0)	1
	Coca-Cola Cup	1 (0)	1
	UEFA Cup	4 (0)	1
	Charity Shield	1 (0)	0
	Total	**40 (0)**	**28**
1997–98	League	15 (2)	2
	FA Cup	6 (0)	5
	Total	**21 (2)**	**7**

31

Index

32